SHAKING THE KALEIDOSCOPE

SHAKING *the*

KALEIDOSCOPE

poems

Kate Kingston

LOST HORSE PRESS
Sandpoint · Idaho

FIRST EDITION

Cover Art: Stephen Linsteadt
Author Photo: Ron Thompson
Book Design: Christine Holbert

This and other fine LOST HORSE PRESS titles may be viewed online at www.losthorsepress.org.

LIBRARY OF CONGRESS CATALOGING-IN-PUBLICATION DATA
  Kingston, Kate.
  Shaking the kaleidoscope : poems / by Kate Kingston.—1ˢᵗ ed.
      p.cm.
  Includes bibliographical references.
  ISBN 978-0-9839975-7-3 (alk. paper)
  I. Title.
  PS3611.I6328S53 2012
  811'.6—dc23
                                    2012033903

for Ron

Table of Contents

What Does Lorca Own?

A garden of tangerine eyes, a parade
of consonants streaming from the balcony,
a city under construction, all the vowels
of history wrapped in a clean white hankie.

When he closes his eyes the Guardia Civil
knock at the door, the garden disappears,
and the pigeons remember a city of horses.

Lorca owns a room full of assonance placating
his pen with *ohs* and *ahs*. He begins to float,
and the room becomes a river, current and undertow.

When he closes his eyes he sees construction
workers, their hands full of hammers; Guardia Civil,
their belts full of sunlight; women in black shoes,

their arms full of vowels. Twenty-six boots cross
the plaza, worn-down heels bring him men
filled with bullets and lime. When he closes his eyes

he sees the stray dog approach his knee, the stray
dog sniff his crotch, the stray dog lick his face.
His fingers tighten around the pen.

Lorca owns the word *Green*.

When he closes his eyes, two skies
          turn chartreuse,
celadon enters like a waft of sunlight.

His favorite word, *Gangrena*.
                    Gangrena.

Shaking the Kaleidoscope I

I cannot recall violence,
only cigar smoke
and the ruined air of traffic,
exhaust
filling my nostrils, cannot
recall pistachios,
the way the shell cracks
between my teeth,
or myself dropping
from a metal
bar chipping my front
tooth on happiness,
the stain of blood in sand,
nothing like the matador
gored in the groin,
so that my lament rises
up next to Lorca
and smells of wet ashes.

Pozo Cañada

Here Spain flattens
into a breath of stale
air. *No mueve nada,*
not even the scorpions.
The limestone
clouds chalk the cavernous
blue with something
like rumors, that low rumble,
nuns at vesper, blue
stain of cobalt bathed
in pastel. I call to tell you
I am thirty-five kilometers
from Albacete,
so you can place your finger
on the map of Spain
and absorb its cinnamon skin,
so you can recall when we
crisscrossed the land
together beneath the iambic
of windmills strumming
their ivory fingers.

After Reading *Romance Sonámbulo*

Verde que te quiero verde.

—*Federico García Lorca*

Living on this river
called Chalk,
has taken a piece
of my turquoise
heart and rendered
it malleable.
Everything I touch
creates a spear
shadow from my elbow
to the tip of my pen.
Chartreuse and celadon
have entered
my retina like orphans.

Burnt orange
and aquamarine
live in the bold
thread of my autumn
shawl, the one that blends
wool with nostalgia
and keeps me humming
gypsy ballads.

Sleepwalkers never
had it so good. Why not
love green as if it were
a dreamer drifting
through the kitchen
with a butterfly net?
Lorca leaves
his penumbra footsteps
on the porch.

Pen of a thousand
cartridges, I offer you
my silk sun,
trailing shadow
like a woman of strong
hair, released.

From the Coast of Almería

The maid covers her mattress in maroon sheets.
Salt rain leaves her balcony in rashes,
and her window takes in mountains, their chain
of granite like undiagnosed profiles
under a cobalt moon and coral sun that match
heat to heat and fill the snail with wounds.

At midnight, the maid unlocks the letterbox, rewinds
the clock, closes the curtain and opens sheets
of papyrus on her desk. She places a song of matches
next to the candle. Her voice flickers like a rash
of ariettas filling the hallway, her moonlit profile
scattering ions. She unlatches the chain

and slips into the stairwell. In her pocket, the keychain
rustles as she presses her fingers to the small wound
at her throat. Summer lightning follows her profile
onto the patio where she wrenches yesterday's sheets
from the line. Rain comes in from Morocco, leaves rashes
of sand on the terrace. Her song cuts through dark matching

her tectonic shift of mood. Even the desert wind is no match
for her high notes. Around her ankle a small chain
engraved with the name of a man who left a star-like rash
smoldering in her memory like a frail piece of thread wound
around her finger. At the window she memorizes sheets
of palm leaves gyrating in wind, a midnight of profiles

moving like sleepwalkers, her own profile
a sea turtle, dark and full of celadon creases that match
the wrinkles in her stained apron, her marooned sheets.
Her silver hair disturbs the dark with its tiny chains
of beaded braids that she twists like a smart wound
over her ears. When she sings his name, tiny rashes

prickle her neck, and stars erupt like a silken rash
in a landscape of poppies and rosebuds. His profile
hums like the sound of bees from the locket she wound
around the bedpost the night she placed wooden matches
next to her candle, the night she unlatched the window chain
to let the brutal dance of fig trees and oleander sheets

enter her wound. She extinguishes the candle and puts matches,
smoking sulfur, next to the rash of peppercorns. Her profile
of silky web and chained rust disappears beneath the sheets.

Shaking the Kaleidoscope II

I cannot recall the sound
of the trolley, its chime
diminished by cathedral bells
nor the prints my knees
left in sand when my mother
lifted me to the car,
cannot recall the taste of honey
nor the voice of the vendor
selling split melons,
nothing like the pigeon,
guttural warble echoing inside
the jojoba, iridescent neck
collecting sunlight, not unlike
this street woman asking
me for *pesetas,* her shoes
as silent as the voice
that refuses. Not violence
to refuse a woman a handful
of coins for her story
spelled out in the sad leather
of her everyday shoes.

Riding the Blue Bus

Granada, Alicante, Molina de Segura, Spanish towns
strung like rosary beads in my mother's hand. *Albacete,*
all the *ahs* of Spain roll off my tongue like the Hail Mary
my mother repeated, her fingers tender on each bead. *Molina
de Segura,* I look for the windmill of safety as radio crackle
infiltrates the Eagle's song, *This could be heaven or this could
be hell,* all the way from Baja to Murcia. *Welcome to the Hotel
California,* repeats itself like the phrase *Now and at the hour
of our death,* which I should never mention while traveling,
nor should I mention the scorpion that raised its spear-like
tail, sensing my bare foot. *Fortuna Archena.* Good fortune
and a chain of arches, how names conjure shapes as we travel
through lemon orchards, their yellow eyes surrounding the bus.
The radio turns to the Monkeys, *I'm a Believer,* and I know
I am. Windmills revolve, change wind to electric. Now Simon
and Garfunkel harmonize, *I am leaving. I am leaving.* The windmills
stay behind touring acres of sky, tender blue *cielo. Tierno
como un beso,* the Bimbo bread sign reads. *Tender as a kiss,*
I translate. Now we pass *Yecla, Jumilla,* like the names of sisters,
then *Mula,* and I think of burlap sacks bulging with oranges
slung over the *mula's* spine. I think of my mother's hips bracing
laundry, grocery bags, the everyday weight of children. But I
am a woman made of chalk and pencils, who carries a notebook
filled with names of Spanish towns, a woman who listens
to the bus radio blow static in one window and out the other.

Huerta de San Vicente

summer home of García Lorca

Tourists swarm like bees singeing
air with perfume. *La huerta* breathes
roses. A garden bride looks at the map.
Its soft corners flap in wind. This day
with lemon blossoms turns brittle.
I breath incense, traffic fumes.
Granada, your profile has shifted.
Two torrents merge beneath a concrete
bridge. The fountain repeats *Federico,
Federico.* I stand in the doorframe
for a photo. Even the trumpet vine
remembers the sound of boots,
the Guardia Civil stepping onto tile.
The wail of a child scorches
the window. A dog's bark bullies
the curtain. In his bedroom, I read
un diálogo de caracoles, words
crossed out, others underscored.
From his pen, one continuous line
forms a man, on his head an ordinary
hat with an ordinary brim. Footsteps
pace the tile, a wood stair creaks
beneath my shoe. Even the window
is restless, tugging at its latch.

Assassination

Did he know that his toe was bleeding amethyst?
Did he open his mouth and place his finger
      on the chartreuse tongue?
Did he call upon his pale blue self to oxidize copper,
      smell tangerines and gutted fish in the market?
Did he wonder how fog lost its pigment
      or how the moon shed its orange husk in daylight?

Did the fringe of his shirt resemble horses
      plunging into the ravine?
Did the space between his eyebrows form bridges
      of tourmaline, his foot recall
      the ache of river?
Did his chiaroscuro laughter turn to dark,
      as little follicles of light touched his ear?
Did his blue lips open?

green

once a deer between two branches
  once rolling hills and spring cliché

    a herd of trees migrating across prairie

once a thought grazing in shade
  an apple shaken too early from its tree

now the broken olive twig
  a river held by concrete, cactus defending its own skin

    a lawn stripped of dandelions

now the wound in Lorca's poem, *la gangrena*
    now the turtle stepping onto highway.

Shaking the Kaleidoscope III

I cannot recall violence,
but one morning my son's face
turned blue. I forced
my own breath into his lungs,
cannot recall the sound of waves
claiming shore or the way
his feet toed-in, only the cadence
of silence, nothing like
the chain of mountain peaks
suffering from lack of rain.
I cannot recall the way a knife
slices coconut into quarter-moon
wedges, cannot recall cleats
biting into cobblestone, nor the bull
lifting his horns to the groin,
the matador spilling onto sand,
nothing like the pomegranate
or the blue face of a child
when his lungs will not pull air,
nothing like exhaust filling
my nostrils or pesetas
dropping into an open palm.

After *La Corrída*

in the Carmona Hotel

The matador hangs his suit of lights on the *balcón,*
as his cigar smoke floats over the *feria* light in a green
haze. *Tapas of albóndigas* and *salchicha* slide to the floor
from the waiter's surprised wrist as the *torero* enters
with his beautiful women dressed in Spanish eyes
and flamenco, their white ruffles escaping to the floor
like released doves. The matador's slim waist, his dance
with the bulls makes the woman tether their hair with high
combs, lace their boots with leather. The *aficionados*
pass photographs of *verónicas* filmed in digital hopes,
a rerun back to the *corrida* where Fandí himself placed six
banderillas in the bull's withers, then placed his hand
on the brow and ran backwards, his feet light as paper,
a ballet in reverse over *las arenas* leading the bull in ritual
across the tamed sands of Almería. *Aficionados* released
Menorcan cocks, and the crowd demanded *música.*
Even the flies were still when Fandí pulled the sword
and pierced the heart in one deliberate stroke. White *pañuelos*
swayed the judge's decision and the *mozo* cut the ears
and tail from the bull, placed them in the hands of children.
Girls wore roses in their hair while bulls churned restless
in the chutes. Rerun back to the bus ride from Veras
to Mojácar, the quiet streets of Garucha on fire
with bold moon and sea spray. Later, after dancing
and chocolate, the *aficionados* let their bodies dissipate
naked in the rhythm of waves breaking, the lift and tug
as each swell released its power in a tidal embrace,
and we watched *la luna* turn masculine before our eyes.

Labyrinth of Moons

Carnival moon trails me home through the alleys
of Granada, unflinching stare, peppercorn
light. Radiance taps the fig trees as they blossom
above the soft bleating of goats. This caramel
moon with cinnamon charm, the one children
call temptation, because it smells like warm
milk with honey. Even the burros lick their lips
and wait for it to fall as it clings to branches,
refuses to ripen. *Sendero* moon trails fireflies
and gypsy moths through a sky crisscrossed by bats,
a cliché galleon passing sailors with its sails
on fire. Another rises through a cornucopia of stars
like a red balloon above the Sierra. Children clap
their hands to welcome its shiny cheeks full of chocolate
and pencils. Piñata moon floats the Andalucía
sky alongside the Flamenco moon, her yellow skirt
lifted, her fingers blinking castanet light. Caustic
moon scorches the Alhambra dark after the guards
have left. Its muscular jaw bullies the stars into pin pricks,
sends tourists down the alley toward the lights
of La Plaza Nueva. Its gold-coin sphere keeps rich men
on their knees. Its sour lemon face keeps children
fogging windows with their sugar breath.

La Playa

Only a handful of us left
on this spare beach. Spanish lunch
has called the sensible
in from the scorch of Mojácar,
but I cannot leave this salt
breath in sea spray. I cannot leave,
so hour after hour I let
shore waves lift and drop me
like some inconsequential
weight, until I believe in time. I am
right up there with the *caracol,*
with the beach pebbles
and shells, doing what I do best,
eroding my sharp edges
into something fine and smooth,
something a child might
glimpse stuck there in the sand
when the tide goes out,
something a child might pick up
and add to her collection.

Shaking the Kaleidoscope IV

I cannot recall the taste
on my tongue when I was saved
by the skin-of-my-teeth, nothing
like a-nick-in-time, the sharp
rasp of tooth against metal
punctuating sand with red, nothing
like the matador lighting his cigar,
the infirmary bed vibrating
under his weight, nothing like
the word *Olé* etched in sand as bells
shake the sky from its reverie
of white distance, nothing like
the dog with no collar sniffing
my left foot, the dog who stole
the eyes of the beggar woman. Pesetas
are not like violence, they make no
sound unless you drop them
into a cup, nothing like the girl pulling
a balloon by the string. Her father
calls, *Marí, ven aquí,* and the balloon
rises to the cathedral spire.

Lorca's Disappearance

It was the way his memory entered the room
like a bell calling villagers to church
through a field of broken pencils,
sorrow from the onslaught of pigeons.

I forgive the man in the black suit coat,
blossom of white in his buttonhole,
a ruin in his voice like melted candles,
waft of hand curling into green light.

A photograph blowing across the plaza
in a country full of olives.

My Hand Through the Keyhole

I give you my hand through the keyhole.
It will cost you a field of stones.
You will pay in fresh cut timothy.
The horse loves me like salt.

I give you my hand in a wicker basket.
It will cost you an ear.
You will pay with timber and sweat.
The fly loves me like salt.

I give you my hand in a book.
It will cost you an alphabet.
You will pay with long vowels.
Words love me like salt.

I give you my hand wrapped in cellophane.
It will cost you a pound of yeast.
You will pay with wheat germ and milk.
Bread loves me like salt.

I give you my hand wrapped in barbed wire.
It will cost you the appaloosa.
You will pay with topaz and smoke.
Jasper loves me like salt.

I give you my hand painted green.
It will cost you eleven ballads bound
in sinew. You will pay in butterflies.
Sleepwalkers love me like salt.

Driving Away

In the rearview I see the whisper
that climbs up my throat past
the ruddy nasturtium of my neck.
I see a dragonfly on my left ear,
a black widow on my right. I see a map
of insects cavorting like jugglers,
their buzz and hiss a pleasure.
On my neck I feel a kiss, in my hair
a cobweb, between my breasts
a garter snake. My waist is girded
with bees, my thigh with ants.
When I look in the rearview, I see
a gravestone, variegated and green,
an olive tree ignited by lamplight.

Lunatic

for García Lorca

One moon left to fall
from your voice of candlesticks
and pomegranates, to hand
over the pencil you write with,
one moon full of persimmon
to break open the shower
of trinkets into the cobblestone ear
of the broom's whisper, to tattoo
its lip on sky's shoulder. One voice
full of spiders and thistle left to harbor
this stolen button, this dime,
this broken comb.

Shaking the Kaleidoscope V

I cannot recall violence,
how it wears a red hat and stands
on the corner selling news,
lives on the beach in corrugated
cardboard, changes its name
to *Passion* and stays out
long after midnight, cannot recall
violence, but by the crack
of my teeth on metal, I knew
the world resonated with chipped
porcelain, that I would go crazy,
have fun with it, shake it up,
and return to the sound of cathedral
bells slicing sky into bite size
pieces, nothing like the woman
on the corner of Canal and Recreo
peeling mangos into ripe moons
that resonate on my tongue.

Concourse A Exhibit

The painting is lovely, but for a security line that people have no choice
to stand in, to see skeletons before they board a flight
is inappropriate for the venue.

—*Airport screener for art exhibits*

Not appropriate to shed bones in the display case,
to calcify water colors, magenta flowering into powder blue,
not appropriate to leave calcite deposits on the glass, nor a water
color image on the brain, not appropriate to brush charcoal rivers
and burial mounds at the feet of deer,
      their tense bodies moving like milkweed
through the Purgatoire, not appropriate while holding your shoes,
your quart baggie of three-ounce liquids, your laptop unsheathed,
keys in a dish, not appropriate to view the river with conquistador
skulls when you walk through the metal detector
      with the eye socket of the skeleton staring back
as you clutch your boarding pass and identification in one hand,
your carry-on in the other, not appropriate to think of bones
when the country is in code orange, to view the structure
that holds it all together, the thighbone connected
      to the hipbone connected to the breastbone,
not appropriate to reveal the rib cage minus heart and lungs
when you wait in line to empty your pockets, to let skulls full of air
and aerodynamics filter into your security quest. Not appropriate
to view pastel ribs tangled in thorn branches,
      deer antlers spiking sky while standing
in your stocking feet, empty shoes in a bin, hair gel in zip-lock,
not appropriate to suggest the skeleton is inside you handing
the boarding pass to the security officer, the skeleton emptying
pockets of coins, stepping into the scanner,
      stepping back into shoes, then taking the hand
of the skeleton child to board the aircraft where the flight attendant
warns to fasten safety belts, not appropriate to smuggle skeletons
past security, skeletons hidden beneath muscle and sinew with teeth,
vertebrae, cranium, inappropriate to view a skeleton before boarding.

Traveling Alone

I walk a road called Recreo, stay overnight

in a city of plazas.

Everywhere the sound of men snoring,

their shaggy hair steaming with vowels.

I walk like a woman who has seen the millennium
spew pomegranates,

false breath, closeted angels, Picasso's bulls.

I melt with the ease of candle wax,

remember an angel named Michael,

how he loved the arch of a woman's foot

and rode down stars.

I can think of nothing better

than to have him return in a boat full of night crickets.

Neruda

brings me a white robe, and we walk toward Mexico,
land of *phantasmagórica.* He brings me *cenote* water
tasting of sacrificial virgins, their palms of spring green.
Neruda brings me eggplant. The sheen of its purple
skin cares about weather. He brings *pasteles,*
café negro, a pitcher of cream, a green orange, *pan dulce.*
He brings Chilean snow, its laughter like a child
on a swing. Neruda brings me a carpet. We explore magic,
a church steeple, the purple of *arco íris,* castle
towers. He explains flight, how to cross my ankles,
center myself so that rising feels like falling. Neruda
brings me a handful of sand fleas, clay jars crawling
with ticks. *You mustn't learn to expect things,*
he explains. He brings a half grapefruit, serrated,
ready for the tongue. It transforms my language. I speak
Portuguese, then a phrase of Italian. He brings
quiet pearls, the breasts of women, street signs, arrows
pointing north. Neruda brings me shadows scaling wall,
a bowl of pomegranates, bees mating in a Mason jar.
He brings a picnic basket, two bottles of wine,
watches me sip alone under a variegated palm.
His hand on the pen, he begins to laugh as if the sea
had said something funny. He brings me a car engine,
just for the sound of acceleration, the taste of exhaust
on my tongue. He brings a sparrow, a dead one,
in his outstretched palm. He reads from his *Book
of Questions.* I listen to the weather of vowels cross his lips,
watch the tiny syllables of moisture lift from his brow.

Rash from the Corn Mold Crepes

for Katherine

She began to itch shortly before daybreak,
but that's what she gets for leaving the security
of homemade soup, and following Mexico's rivers,
those little stethoscopes of the heart,
where reed alphabets tangle with water lilies,
where Neruda's stories turn the river to poems.
This rash travels through her rush of dreams
while she tackles daybreak with a plume
in one hand, Mexico fever in the other. She too
must think the river a poem, as she presses
her ear to its uncertain water full of consonant
microbes. Even the stones have come down
with irrational fever and Katherine's song of despair
can't get to the heart, though her paddle
dips river water as the moon's thread continues
its legacy, hemming dusk to daybreak. Stars
weight sky, brighten Orion's belt, while helium
fingers draw the bow, quiver the length of arrow.

When I Clap

My right hand reaches for the feather of memory
that fell from my mother's hat as she bent to get out
of the car, down tugged away on wind, not unlike
the pigeon, roosting now above the church door, satisfied
with alcove. Everything I touch is the texture of oven bread,
round like my mother's voice as I teach her conversation again.
The scent of *empanadas* lingers in the blue opal earthstone
of her earring when she leans to say *Goodnight, God bless,*
until morning, but now, I say the words first because she
has forgotten the sound the fire truck makes outside our window.
What's that? she asks, her palms pressed to her ears.

My left hand smells of the street dog I just stroked
and fed a scrap of bread. His eyes follow me, food to mouth.
He is only the dog smell clinging to my sleeve. His cold nose
pokes my hand, my bare knee, my crotch. When I open my palm
to strike him, he turns to me, the one he will not bite, the one
he will smell again and again. I've never touched that cloud
outside the plane window, though I've wanted to ever since
I was a child and looked up to the dinosaur, the whale, a giant face,
all vapor, all change, all the promise of rain above my head.

I've lost the questions. Each word like a hundred shards
scuttles across the floor. It is not like the cup, glass, china plate.
It makes no sound, but a flavor hovers from the wreckage: onion,
garlic, cinnamon, *cebolla* with a scent of burning underbrush.
When I reach for the apron, tie the knot behind my back,
the memories fall into the braided hair of my daughter. My palms
knead bread, shape loaves, set trays in ovens. My nails
are softened by white flour that clings, leaves fingerprints
on everything I touch. When I bring my hands together they are
not the *empanada.* They are not folded with the blend of *atún,*
cebolla, pimiento. They are not hands that seal at the edges.
They are not hands that stay together. They are not hands.

I've touched the answer, but unlike the dog, it left. Even answers
chase pigeons until they lift towards the church alcove. You can't hear
flapping wings until the bird is above you, and these pigeons think
I have bread. They gather. They coo. They fly startled when I celebrate
my open palms in their direction. It is not the sound of snow. It is not
the sound of rain. It is not weather. It is a broom lapping cool stones.
It is my mother cleaning the patio.

Climbing

las ruinas de Chichén Itzá

Their bruised skulls found in the *cenote* tell us the women
were struck, pushed over an edge into the sweet water
of this underground river. It's easy to imagine them piecing
together a thatched roof or rocking children in the cool
sling of a hammock, and when the sun was highest, shooing
iguanas from flat stones where they placed laundry
to dry. It's harder to imagine them on the stone steps at noon
under a sun that was god and calendar, praying for rain,
giving children for rain. I climb these same steps, too narrow
for my feet, too steep for my spirit. I press my fingers
to grey stone, hand over hand, to calm myself against height.
At the top an altar connects to ritual, heart cut from the body.
Chacmool, semi-reclining, still holds a sacrificial tray,
paled white under the same sun. Touching porous stone,
I try to absorb the promise of an exotic god: jaguar or serpent.
When I don't understand the silence beneath my fingers,
I step back, take pictures, center an altar between two pillars
that once supported a roof. I've climbed such a short way
to the top of this pyramid and will go down the same steps,
lowering my center of gravity one foot at a time,
clutching the cabled rail to steady my descent.

Turistas: El Museo De Las Momias

Guanajuato, Mexico

We meet the mummies, face to face, but weren't expecting
them to call out to us, their lips stretched, petrified in groans,
gritos, gruñidos. The curator explains as skin dehydrates,
lips pull away from teeth, so we witness these mouths shaping
wide vowels, *Ohs* and *Ahs* frozen in torment. He moves us
along to two unearthed doctors, an oriental woman, children
dressed as *santos,* one in purple and gold, a rosary braided
through toes, perfect thumbs the width of bailing twine,
fingers laced on the lily's stem, petrified petals. A mother
with the wound above her womb is displayed next to her embryo,
the Caesarian stillborn. Another woman shields her eyes
to thwart the blow revealed in her skull. The curator continues
his monologue while we observe intact eyelashes, beards,
and pubic hair, hermetically sealed behind glass. We shuffle
past line after skeletal line, as if to discover some clue
in *la boca,* that open tunnel where no noise escapes, some clue
in *la lengua,* the parchment tongue that once supported a voice.

Aztec Exhibit: *The World of Motecuhzoma*

I put on earphones and walk through arches
into subdued light. I hear macaws, mallets
shaping wood, running feet against earth,
women bartering. On a wall taxes are woven
into debts: turkey feathers, blue beads,
chocolate. The voice says, *Turn left, approach*
the glass case in the middle of the room.
I turn into a face listening to the same voice
and step lightly on a foot. A goddess carved
from granite gives birth to corn. The voice
says *Tlazolteotl, eater of filth,* because she listened
to the wrongs. My fingers ache for the stone,
but we are separated by glass and a sign
that says *Do Not Touch.* I listen to rain fall,
women chant, men rise up steps, the sound
of Tlaloc accepting. I hear the knife pressed
to flesh. Chacmool absorbs blood into cool stone.
Huitzilopochtli leans forward. I hear sun
sweep a courtyard, the rustle of her clothes
as she picks up feathers and places them
next to her skin. I hear seed take shape
into child, moon break into parts, her body
pieces of stone unearthed and all the signs say
Do Not Touch. I listen to horse's hooves and breath
and leather shift beneath the weight of armor,
the sound of gold melting, feathers falling,
and Doña Marina talking as her voice erases
all the footprints. The sound of smallpox gathers
beneath skin. The strong, bracing silence leans
against the wall; the empty, hollow silence
allows us to walk through. The still, petrified
silence crouches like the goddess in childbirth
—a frozen sound, only beginning to thaw; the sound
of stone, when finally I press my ear to the glass.

In the Beginning

I want to read God tonight,
     turn the white page of his left foot,
find my name tattooed just below the ankle.
     I want to read him
like a *Book of Questions* or *A Song of Despair,*
     then ride on the motorcycle
he left in El Jardín, the one resting on its kickstand, two girls
     leaning curious over the handlebars.

I want to ride over the back tire,
     singe my leg on exhaust,
proof I've ridden with my hands
     wrapped around his waist,
ride with him when he trips the starter
     and leans into curves,
our helmets bobbing through pedestrians
     on Calle Jesus, his eye
out for young souls, stalkers all of us,
     in his image and likeness.

San Miguel and Wolf Creek

after 9/11

If you want me to break away from fear
I have to put my boots on, trample a few things
like that CNN reporter. I have to cancel
my airline tickets and ignore the man with the red
cane who taps my ankle as he passes my plaza bench,
then continues tap-tapping his way to the cathedral
door. If you want me to break away from fear,
I have to stand in line, and this line leads to the chairlift,
the closest I'll ever come to ascension. It lifts me
swinging above the snow-glaze, a single cable
my connection to ecstasy. As I tell you this,
the pigeon struts up to my toe, pecks it like a kernel
and flutters away. Oh, that flight could be so easy!

I have to put my boots on, not the cowboy
but the snow kind, the black flexible neoprene
that wraps above my ankle in thick comfort
with laces as long and seductive as the siren's
voice, her promise of ecstasy just before slipping
under surf, while here in the plaza, two girls
run in circles, pretending they are pigeons,
yelling—no, singing—*Vuela-vuela, vuela-vuela.*
This day is so full of ecstasy, I want to return
to the mountain, strap the snowboard
to the bottom of my feet, secure the heel and arch,
ride until powder rises up like ocean spume
onto my forehead layering me in white,
until I rise from the drift as certain as the pigeon,
until I too am singing, *Vuela-vuela, vuela-vuela.*

Even the clowns have joined us: red noses,
pink frizzed hair, motorcycles, a band, balloons,
horses, *los Tres Reyes*—green, blue, gold—followed

by *bomberos,* firemen, and the children
who have waited so long to be caught up in this gyration
migrating toward El Jardín. *Vuela-vuela, vuela-vuela.*
Yet even above the ecstasy of their voices, the siren
breaks through, a reporter scribbles, much like me,
into an open notebook, the fireman leans to pull
his boots on, and I ride again over Alberta Peak,
drift off, free-fall, catch air. *Vuela.*

In the event of an emergency

think of oxygen masks as halos,
seatbelts as bungee cords,
tray tables as butterflies,
think of the flight attendant as Wonder Woman,
the pilots as Laurel and Hardy,
think of the person next to you as scent-free,
no tinge of emanating decay.
Think of air as water, how it floats the body.

In the event of an emergency,
think how inertia presses each body
into the seat back
until there are one-hundred-twenty-two hearts
struggling for space.
Think of oversize carry-ons, overhead bins,
the cockpit, the exit.
Think of blue, think of cold, think of infinity
right here, outside the window.

Mayan Riviera Wedding

Mother-of-the-bride tells the story

The bride yawns, leaves the sorbet, filet, lobster,
escapes shadow-like toward her groom,
toward candles and confetti, toward their next touch.
Guests throw shoes in the fire pit, dance
to the smell of burning suede, leather, plastic, sisal,
releasing their pent-up spirits. Oh, how they dance,
their sassy feet pounding gaiety into earth
on the 21st parallel. Who knows what longitude
they discover, as they sway to marimba and smoke,
their teeth and irises reflecting blue flame.

When salt water gets in my nostrils and rip tide
gets in my soul, I remember my daughter in Yalku
sunning on grey rock, as the groom snorkeled
around her little island of mangrove and coral.
Her one open eye followed the tip of his blue snorkel
as he fluttered by underwater. So easily she slipped
from her rock, merged with him in one silver flick
of fin. Why do I think of teeth, when it is the legs
that propel her through the lagoon bubbling with tourists?

I tell the taxi driver, *Vimos un cocodrilo,* then ask,
¿Son peligrosos? He laughs as he glances in the rearview,
my daughter in the backseat, wind slicing dark hair.
They won't hurt if you don't touch, he smiles,
his one eyetooth visible, overlapping the others, so that
when he speaks, I think only of teeth. But the coati
is another story—its long snout almost took my finger
when I reached to part its fur. *¡No toque!*
the keeper yelled. I should have learned that by now.
It's like trying to touch the heart, the way
it can turn, snap off a finger, and that constant flow
of venom percolating just inside the rib cage.

Alone I explore the *cenote,* snorkel its underground river,
splash through caverns, place of Mayan sacrifice.
I paddle to a fat stalagmite, hoist myself onto limestone,
pull a vigil candle and waterproof matches from my hem.
Blind fish surface as the wick's lisp and sputter
provoke good air. Ceiling bats, *murciélagos,* struggle
with light, not unlike my daughter—her complicated veil,
its lace teeth catching on doorknobs, on coat hangers.

I begin a new altar, a piece of stalagmite wrapped in kerchief.
My new chant, *murciélago, murciélago,* a word like a chalice
holding one of each syllable. My vigil, my mantra, my stalactite
santos cling to limestone ceiling. My daughter's vows, so like
a stream of *murciélago* wings—erratic spiral, sonar drift.

My Mother's Footsteps

I'm not following you to the loom. I don't hear your footsteps
on the stairs. Oranges and tangerines aren't ripening
in these branches, green globes lightly dusted.

I don't hear Zapotec syllables flit through trees
like kaleidoscopic birds, or the sigh of Magda as she bends
for water. I don't count meters of hose coiled around pipe

or hear water's maniacal tumble from spigot to bucket,
don't hear your footsteps on the stairs or the embroidered light
filtering through banana leaves. I don't see the weaver

with her indigo thread, her patio stones, her *huaraches,*
or see Magda cleaning the *comal* where last night she charred
blue corn over coals, Magda who turned away

when I asked for a photo. I don't hear your footsteps
on the roof, on the street or blue stairs. I don't count
the pomegranate clusters or sheets cascading in breeze,

their fluidity tattooed in wind. I don't see Magda carry
the straw basket over her shoulder into the alley,
don't hear your footsteps on the roof, under the stairs,

or across the patio. I don't hear geraniums split
into red blossoms, nor do I flinch at the trigger of fireworks
as if the sky has been shot and is falling.

My corner of the garden is dark and ravenous
—a tangled cacophony of roosters, brooms, brays,
and unnamed birds that just sing and sing.

Framing a Piece of Ruin

Eva lives here, feeds chickens in her flowered housedress,
and in her yard assembles two bathtubs, each with a Virgin statue
muddled in plastic carnations. Here the mint bird speaks
in romance language and sweet peas are braided so thick the tongue
marbleizes. Cedar branches like a rain of tentacles interlace
her fence, a cadence of weathered wood. In the shed, a feed pan
full of pebbles, a yellow rope like a withered snake coils in a bramble
of barbed wire and bailing twine. Cottonwood bark splits
into a woman's face. She peers out from the tree scar, like a siren
singing the timber songs. Through a séance of haloed leaves,
sunrise crystallizes into orange salt, wind worms dangle from spiral
webs. Chollas spiked with magenta surround her barn, as a rash
of sunlight warms the adobe wall tumbled into heaps. A robin
steals the last chokecherry. I peer through the cellar door,
decayed cedar and stucco that once protected her winter apples.

The Glass

slips from my hand, leaves the scent of cocoa butter
        clinging to my fingers,
    that indulgent flavor
        that attracts bees, bears, children, men.

The glass has fallen,
            leaving my hand clutching the dried flowers,
    the scent of chamomile-yellow
        rusted to my knuckles.

A kaleidoscope of shards
            shuttles over tile, hushed
    like words whispered,
            their meaning splitting and dividing.

Sound rises like liquid smoke
            from the linoleum,
    so like my father's image.
            His amber form slips from the photograph,

floats transparent
            from eye level to the coppery light of the ceiling fan,
    while miniature spears
            radiate between myself and the refrigerator.

The glass has fallen
            like the beehive above the porch swing,
    how I swung the bat just to hear bees swearing,
                chaos in the dry summer air.

I Cannot Name this Place

I live in the plaza of pigeons—orange necks, turquoise
feathers, pink claws tracking the grey rasp of cobblestone.
I live with cathedral bells, how they harbor the voices
of saints, the mewing of kittens. Wind enters like a rumor
tugging at the pages of my notebook, reminds me
of the swamp where I buried my feet in black mulch
up to my calves while a snapping turtle buried her eggs
in sand. I care about winter and my own mother hooked up
to the machine of morphine good-byes, but it is my daughter
who paces the floorboards. I want to circle the plaza,
walk into sunshine and traffic on Calle de Insurgentes, smell
acres of corn roasting. I want to taste licorice and wear
taffeta. I want the sound of engines to stomp out the ashes
of a memory where my daughter wrestles, her throat gripped
by that crazed boy who dragged her up a flight of stairs
by her neck. Her cousin saved her, ran to her own mother
and said, *Jason's hurting her,* while I was out alpine skiing
the slopes, blue Utah sun in my hair. Now she has become
the asphalt I dream on, that warm place under the plaza bench
where I store my cigarettes and empty bottle, the place
where pigeons never enter. Their cooing fills me with stones.

The Dream Turtle

surfaces just long enough
for me to see diamonds glued
to its emerald shell, like a sea bracelet,
paddling out to open ocean. Its head
is a cedar stalk, posed and certain,
towing a clothesline through water
with my father's wardrobe trailing behind,
clothes my sister boxed up and sent
to Goodwill before I had a chance
to sort through embroidered hankies,
wool socks, flannel shirts. The turtle swims
through ice melt, and I follow,
stroking one hand forward, then another,
cupping my fingers like a webbed paddle,
the body so like a boat, so like a turtle.
With each stretch of arm,
I reach for my father's clothing, the desire
to feel cloth between my fingers,
something tactile to pull into my hands,
to pull over my shoulders. Wools, cottons,
polyesters, tiny stitches that hold us together,
each shirt its own conversation with skin.
But the turtle senses my presence
and submerges, tugging the ivory shimmer of cloth
to the bottom. I wait, floating above,
because I know everything there is to know
about resurfacing, how even a dream turtle
has to come up for air.

Woman Resting

Teotitlán del Valle, Mexico

I have been waiting days to move
to the hammock, to drift
beneath the white portal into a white
dream delineated by black
ink.
      Above me, the green tree
full of green grapefruit and a cluster
of yellow birds. My sky sways
with palm leaves and wingspan.
Footsteps approach
like a lullaby.
      In the distance a child
wails blue syllables and the rooster
releases another *quiquiriquí.*
I sketch their sounds on paper
alongside the corrugated bray
of burro.
      The hammock swings
in the key of G. I am surrounded by tuning
forks and pomegranate blossoms.
I call this place
Granada.
      Lull is the word that comes
to mind. *Lull* says the wood smoke, *lull*
says the sheet on the line, *lull* says
the loom's shuttle tapping wool strands
of indigo and cochineal
into the snug fit
of weft.

Sometimes the name for gold dye
escapes me, so I put down the pen, feel
the rhythm of my body as if I too
am a leaf lulled by breeze,
as if I too am held to the branch
by a nub of stem.

History of My Body

Once this body went into treason, the flat-chested girl
pushed Willie Wall into the thorn bush, and never
stopped riding her pogo stick up and down the driveway
until her brother broke it. The history of this body
is the angel in snow working her arms and legs in long
slashes. The history of this body is like breaking up
a jigsaw puzzle, then letting the pieces float in the river.
Have I told you I'm the hero of this body? I'm as
fluid as water spilling into the boat. I could save you,
but first, you almost have to drown. Once a botfly
laid eggs in this thigh. Hatched larvae trekked
pink stripes across my skin, newborn veins radiating
from the mother egg. The history of this body
has a housefly in its ear, buzz ricocheting like geometric
lace. Take this history back to the tonsillectomy,
back to ice cream in its swollen throat, back to the way
these lips enter a room full of men. Take this ear,
a barrage of spider veins trapping sound. History
of my body inhales secondary smoke from my father's cigar,
inhales primary perfume from my mother's neck, inhales
the broken leaves of autumn crushed beneath my boot.
That pile of minuscule hands pries at the lawn
until I sweep them into a heap and plow through
like a sorceress with conical hat and faithful broom.
This body remembers trick-or-treat, its Snicker bars
and bruised apples. This body remembers the way dried leaves
scratch the skin when I somersault into the pile
of tattooed veins—oak, elm, maple—then wrap myself
in a sarong of silver water. Inside this body, flies buzz,
this body with cake on its tongue.

Sorcery

At dinner Lucinda says I'm a *bruja*.
Our friends believe her and fondle
the stones in their pockets. It's true --
a certain root of witchery crawls up my spine.
I am full of nettle and dormant mice.
The morning harbors distinct white clouds,
some so wide I whisper *wingspan*
and think of all the jets that have carried me
over oceans without a single complaint.
It's no longer safe to fly alone.

A brisk séance is good for the soul, like
tap-dancing with the dead, how their bones
ring like castanets from rock to rock,
as I leap and gyrate through blue spruce
telegraphing honesty. I don't want
to return to the garden, to the pitch fork
of Lucinda's tongue raised like a weapon.
I am hoping only for a lake smooth
enough to skim, a lake called *Glass*
for its mirror-like deceit.

What spell have I cast on the continent?
In the Heartland, corn is drowning. In the West
homeless clouds drift with nothing to spare.
Their wispy arms span the sky like water
gypsies. Sometimes I insist on flood, the town
immersed up to its knees. Sometimes I hear
crows dispatch messages in the juniper.
I translate their songs, then ride my motorcycle
over Raton Pass into New Mexico. I shift
gears and run the red lights. Behind me I hear
sirens. Wind lifts my hair, reveals
the blackbirds tattooed to the back of my neck
as if someone had just opened a pie.

Hallowe'en

I take black riding boots from the trunk
to make the witch in me complete.
I am the only sister with feet small enough,
big enough. I dump acorns from the toe,
shake them to be sure, and pull
stiff polished leather to my knee cap.
On the street I pass other witches
with star-studded capes, dime store wands,
their straw-sewn brooms, but I am the only witch
with my mother's boots, their sound
against pavement, ringing heel
and snapping toe of each step up and down
long sidewalks of neighbors
with my paper sack held out for coins,
apples, colored sugar in wrappers. I scale
picket fences, race through backyards,
up garage steps, through hallways, trailing
the skeletal outline of heel and toe
across linoleum. I hear the rusted hinge
as my mother opens the broom closet to sweep
away. I hear the rusted hinge as I open
the trunk to crawl in, tell stories to spiders, bats,
squirrels, whatever happens to share
this dark haven accessible by tiny slits
just under the eaves. I've found their webs,
their dung, their acorns, so I know
they exist. I pull the riding boots
from my feet, bits of damp moss, gravel,
garden snails clinging to the heel.
I lay them side-by-side in deep folds
of black cape, place them in the trunk, know
they'll wait the whole year for my return.

Finger-Birds

I grew up in a kitchen full of cutting boards,
the kind you pull out and leave out all night
with noodles drying in chalky flour.
I'd sit under these, my sky a wooden lid,
my space small and isolated, watching
the nylon legs of my mother, her hem
of blue gingham move from drawers to sink
to stove and back again. One Sunday,
after church, I crouched there with my sister's
new white gloves changing my hands
to finger-birds that would flutter and dive,
and fly away the length of my arm. I hid
at knee level from my mother's eyes,
while Mary cried into her own bare hands
on the back steps. With each sob she peeled
the wallpaper away, strip after long narrow
strip, then fell asleep with her head propped
against sepia swirls of dried paste
that my mother had dabbed and brushed
to hold pastel ballerinas in arabesque
above our heads. My mother calls to tell me
I forget things now, but today asks
for the chicken recipe. I want to go back,
place my hands in the yellow gloves, scour
her porcelain sink, wring soap water
from dish rags, place lemon rinds and orange
husks with compost. Instead, I listen
to snow fall on snow, several inches, this Sunday,
that I had planned to set onions underground.
I pull leather gloves creased with black soil
over my knuckles, brush snow away, crouch
over row after row of damp earth, pressing
each bulb of papery skin into soil.

Dusting

With a gentle rhythm Teresa erodes
the layers built up with waxes and soaps
until she is down to bare wood
and remembers her neighbor, the one
who gave her this table, a wedding
present. Saturday mornings, watching
Road Runner and Wile E. Coyote,
she straddled the heavy arm of his chair
until he tickled her so hard she fell
into his lap laughing in the luxury
of his fingers, his attention, until one day
his hand slipped below the waist
of her jeans.

Lemon oil seeps into the wood, the rag,
the pores of her right palm. When she rises
to release curtains from their little hooks,
the scent of polish halos her fingers.
She searches the seam, hem, until she finds
a label:

> *Wash Delicate Cycle,*
> *Little or No Ironing Required.*

After he left she looked for her mother
and found her in the kitchen slicing noodles
from flat dough. When she asked to help,
her mother said she was too young for knives,
so she just watched the deft fingers
prepare soup from boiled chickens.
Beside her, she drew circles in chalky flour
as the redness faded until it was only a marble,
wedged solid in the round heel of her belly.

Onions

I sink my hand in the oak barrel,
pull up handfuls of one-inch reds
and press their hardness into the tilled soil
with my thumb. I wait for shoots
so tiny they could be grass. Onions for *salsa,*
for salad, for stew, onions for eating
later on. Between bread with *jalapeños*
and cold cuts, stuffed into the baggie,
opened at noon, swallowed but lingering,
like memories—how my sister slipped
past the bouncer to sip beers for a quarter,
to watch Mike push dollar bets in his pocket,
dive in the channel sending security men
on a night-long search of the opposite shore.
These layers of skin, thick, peelable,
getting to the heart of one makes me cry.
I chop instead of peel, find it hard
to keep my hands on something so pungent.
How we bargained *huaraches*
from beach vendors, softened their leather
in sea water on our way to the open market,
an afternoon watching tourists pale
as they caught sight of the pig's head on a stick,
pink hooves placed underneath.
Now with salt water on my cheeks,
I am in the kitchen setting corn and onions
on the table with real butter and salt,
like they served at summer fests
back in Wisconsin. How Mary wrestled
me to the sidewalk if I sang the kissing song
with Jimmy's name and hers. When we got up,
disentangling ourselves, the scratches
always felt cool and open on my skin.

Experimenting with LSD

after the poetry reading

You promise me my first trip. I leave breathing the color blue,
smell the pink of your aftershave. Monkeys peek through keyholes.
Your smile beams, a cavern of white elephants. An ivory train
gyrates in your mouth like a word caught in stutter. I smell rainbows
drifting from your ears. I taste the pith of Credence, *Bad Moon
on the Rise,* and hold up a chandelier of champagne, my hand dazzling
five digits scorching a background of lyrics, *memories and elephants* . . .
In this parade we are touching like a lullaby, the room full of dozing
zebras. Their black and white stripes followed us here from the poetry
reading, trying to impress on us the importance of a line. I recognize
a circus when I eat one, and this circus promises me the man
on the flying trapeze. I am in the big top swinging, an acrobat tasting
somersaults midair, hovering over the *ahs* of the crowd while you
metamorphose into a clown. I press my tongue to your cheek,
taste Double Bubble. To make me laugh, you ride across the room
on a pencil, bursting like a firecracker when you touch it to paper.
My hair takes on the sheen of licorice. I make a wish for spotted
zebras, their marshmallow muzzles pink as cotton candy. I ride
the elephant up State Street, amber glow drizzling in my ear. Bees
buzz from their light bulb nests, leave me electric. I breathe magenta
and purple. You race past me on your rock-candy motorcycle.
We are headed to the dorm with its spool of clowns tying balloons
into wiener dogs. Together we sound like hornets. We smell
like sassafras and root beer. Even the lion tamer is jealous.

Kiss

The one-page love poem begins and ends with a kiss.
But what about that space between kisses, like meeting
at the festival of San Gerónimo—pole climbers, Indian
jewelry, flute music, and later, the hike up Devisadero
Trail through foothills. We substituted grapes for kisses.
Our lips were happy then, and the chipmunks gathered
the seeds we spit. Dinner at Lambert's, we substituted
Cabernet for kisses. Our lips turned purple and the cook
laughed over a shot of Jack Daniels. You gave twenty
dollars to a man with a hard-luck story and we drove
toward blankets scattered on the floor. A piano stood
in the corner, untouched, watching us as the scent
of skin filled our nostrils and our hands swept
the surface of each other. In the morning we studied
light and ventured into a day filled with bicycles, gold
leaves. We recognized art in a city of tourists. A magpie
rehearsed in the cottonwood. That was the day men carried
bales of alfalfa to the barn, left the stubble to field mice.
Before you got in your truck, you placed the basket of green
chilis on the hood to free your arms. As you pulled away,
the lilt of road dust left its trace on my lips.

In your next letter

I wish you'd say
where you are going and what you are doing.

—*Elizabeth Bishop*

Remind me of Spain, its olive coast, its rugged breath,
a gypsy with sky in her pocket, snatches of poppies, voices
of street women. Remind me of Spanish weddings,
how the white train sweeps the floor and the bride's shoulders
are no longer homeless. In your next letter remind me
of Marrakech where the camels found homes and the street urchin
led us to soup, of Formentera where the bicycle
slid into the ditch, wounding my left breast, and the cabin,
chinks fallen away, wind like a transient, the guest
no one wanted, and the view, always through a crack.

In your next letter place a postage stamp over my name, press
your tongue to the return address, list all the possibilities
of a wedding in the woods. In your next letter name a child after me,
keep her free from nightmares. Keep her. In your next letter
tell me the way a single raindrop meets the window, the way
you carry my shoes to the bed. We left mildew and oak leaves,
moved West, apples in the glove box. We left creameries
and breweries, moved onto prairie. Silence rose up like beggars,
until we tossed coins into grass and sang them away.

Love Story

You have always been one to collect things
—fossils, postage stamps, baseball hats, buffalo nickels—
because searching is an art that started shortly after birth
to fill long evenings on the farm when books weren't enough,
and the cows had been milked for the second time in a day.
The long sleeves of flannel shirts hung waiting in your closet
for the day you would leave and move to the desert.
You spent years digging coal from Emery County dirt,
so we could live in that house on the edge of Utah,
watch our breath dissipate over the San Rafael.
We lived in silences so long, I dreamed they were tunnels,
and now, I have given up trying to recognize you
in the pale stain of desire, how touch becomes so familiar
the skin expects it and surprise is an element
buried as deep as the bituminous veins of Emery.

My fingers reach for the faint stickiness of cream
that has dried on your skin, but it is your arms I am after,
the thick possibility of being held in summer,
while the cows low and shuffle their restless feet
as their milk comes down. If I called you *Beloved*
to your face, a curious eye would blink, olive green
and full of trees. Tonight I will tell you
about the bobcat that saunters through my garden
with fur like silver ore, because I believe
there is flannel in all of us. Even now, standing here
at the edge of desert with both feet planted,
I watch the moon lose her tangerine ink, watch her scale
octaves higher as the Bookcliffs blacken,
and her sphere fades to a pale yellow, soft and unobtrusive
as a street lamp breathing phosphorescence.

My Mother's Dance

This is one of those moments I play
and replay, an old movie camera clicking
its teeth, as the tape shuttles her image
across a paper screen. She rises
from her chair as if on cue, and while the band
tangos, her arms claim their space, neck
to fingertips undulating like beach waves.
She weaves a two-step in and out of our tables,
her hand caressing air, then the chin
of my brother, my husband's shirt collar,
the lace elbow of my niece. We all feel
the quiver of strings as she cha-chas, two-steps,
tangos. Her eyes never seek the floor.
When the film ends, its tail flapping loose,
I switch to rewind and watch my mother
spin backwards onto the original spool.

Later I turn open the white pages. My pen
leaves notes: the color of her dress, smell
of her gardenia, pulse of her wrist,
size of her shoe. My pen takes on the rhythm
of waves touching shore, closing distance
between water and sand. I string vowels
to consonants, choreograph each pirouette,
each arabesque of letter to letter across page.
My words are a waltz pacing emotion,
a tango looping around faces that stare
as my mother takes the microphone
from my father's hand and says, *I can't speak
but I sure can dance.* Her body sashays
toward the dinner tables where we gather
our years around us like secret stones
in a child's pocket.

Fish like Angels

shopping with my daughter

I fill your hands with fluorescent fish, the ones
we buy at Wal Mart, carrying them home
in plastic bags. I notice their reflection
in your fingernails, the shimmer of tail and fin.
The angelfish is your favorite, how it fans
translucent wings and ascends through water.
The current is its home. And just last Sunday,
you described the angels you now see
behind Trinity Hall. *Some as small as leprechauns,*
you said, as we sat under the gazebo eating
peaches just fallen from the tree, peaches
not far enough from the branch for bruises.
I believed in angels once, St. Michael, St Gabriel,
the fallen St. Lucifer, and all those childhood
Saturdays in the confessional repeating *Bless Me
Father,* then stretching sin just for the part
about forgiveness. I no longer believe
in transparency, though I watch the checkout girl
lift the bag eye level to catch the flicker
of tails in refracted light. In the parking lot,
we dash through downpour, then watch the sun
ricochet prisms through a field of chrome.
We drive home through puddles, accelerate
just to hear the hiss of water beneath tires,
just to catch the wild arch of prism in the rearview,
how it rises behind us like double fins, then careens
back into shimmering pools on purple asphalt.

Albino King Snake

Only the heads tell us there is more than one. Some press
their bodies flat to glass, others coil into themselves.
The owner pulls out drawers marked *Hibernation*
and tells us about the fifty others sleeping in the basement,
waiting for spring when he will warm them with light,
put males and females together. We should come back then,
because the babies are cheaper and the twenty-six dollars
my son has wrapped in his wallet can't buy half a snake now,
so we just hold them. The King Snake slides through our palms
and into shirt sleeves as if we were roots and caverns.
We feel the dry, soft skin, a flow of muscle with no bone,
no angle, nothing sharp but the color, black-banded
against white, and the tongue like soft whiskers sensing air,
tasting direction. Then he lifts an Albino King from the drawer,
its eyes pink, and its flesh the color of my son's own pale
forehead pressed to glass as he watches the white mouse
disappear, whole, alive, head-first.

Argil: Pure Clay

I want a page that will split open like a thousand
daughters, spilling dreams and pencils,
like water breaking from the womb.
Argentiferous liquid crosses stones;
the waterfalls begin their arduous journey.

This daughter I name Forest Green.
I measure each line in her palm the day she is born.
Her hand grows until it is strong enough
to pull her into the saddle, tender enough
to feel pressure between the rein
and the bit.
Even leaves follow her.

Another daughter gathers yucca with a steel trowel,
breaks into the earth just deep enough
to extract the root.
She boils it with sugar and honey over a cedar fire,
spreads a jelly so clear and thin
I recognize her sepia photograph on toast.

Don't I know what it means to feel the rush of afterbirth
on a naked thigh,
to catch the hazel glint of a daughter's eye,
the stampede of hooves
shimmering in the spectrum's iris?

This daughter memorizes all the parts of horses,
marries young, travels islands with names like Cariacou.
She returns taller and long-haired,
sixty-three tiny braids swing from her skull,
the tiny cackle of porcelain beads,
rustle against each other as she crosses a room.
This one turns a shoulder
like a key in a lock, the tiny *click*.

This daughter trims the new buds of prickly pear
from its history of spiked palms.
Its auburn blood stains the knife
as she culls each spine from the areole,
Under the kitchen light, she tosses chopped cactus,
cilantro, marjoram. She sprinkles salt,
crushes feta between her fingers.

Don't I know what it means to stand in the driveway,
to wave the white handkerchief,
to feel the stampede of hooves shimmering?
Don't I know what it means to recognize the hazel glint,
to feel the rush of afterbirth on a naked thigh?

This daughter chews the tips of sleepy grass
to prove it makes horses drowsy.
She buys an Arabian mare and a second-hand saddle,
rides the length of South Shore, up Bon Carbo road.
Barefoot and hatless,
she crosses the Purgatoire after the first snake,
its dry rattle trailing arid heat.

This daughter dyes her hair blue, smokes blue cigarettes,
tints the icing, the eggs, the cookie dough, the milk
with a drop of blue food coloring.
She paints herself blue,
sapphire fingernails, turquoise toenails, porcelain lips,
aqua elbows, violet ankles
a peacock blue navel, magenta breasts
a delft blue pelvis.
When she stands at the horizon
she's invisible, blue sky at her back.

Gravity

Sometimes you slip when you swing out over the lake,
        your fingers clenching a frayed rope, your legs dangling.
The cold splash. Water up your nose. Or on the frozen pond
        you slip on the tail of crack-the-whip, your figure skates
gliding out from under. Sometimes you slip when you balance
        just so on the kitchen stool reaching for the cinnamon
rolls Aunt Ila tucked behind the saucers, or you slip when
        you cross the metal pole in the closet, hand over hand,
you slip and land in a pile of rubber boots with metal clasps
        that jangle and scratch the back of your legs.
Sometime you slip when you cross the monkey bars, your front tooth
        cracking on metal as you fall, or when you follow
your brother and Eugene up Big Hill, you slip and gravel
        bites into your knees, so they know you are there,
but they let you climb with them anyway, if you carry the bottles
        of Coke in your pack and don't tell anyone.
Sometimes you slip when you walk from the church to the rectory
        with a basket of donuts for the priest, you slip
leaving streaks of pink frosting in the blades of grass. Sometimes
        you slip when Bobby holds your hand
and roller skates around the rink, you slip and feel the wooden floor
        heave and buckle under his laughter as he reaches
with both hands to pull you up, or when you drive the icy roads
        of Wisconsin with your new license, you slip and the Chevy
spins into white powder. Sometimes you slip when you descend
        the backstairs with a suitcase headed for college
or when you walk down the aisle, everyone in town watching
        the back of your head. Sometimes you slip when you pull
your daughter across a white field on her new sled or when
        you lean over the edge of a canoe on Silver Lake, you slip
in over your head and almost drown from laughing so hard,
        water up your nose.

Sometimes you slip when the trail up to Devil's Causeway
is muddy, you slip and fall back to the trailhead,
to your red Subaru parked in the shade of a willow. Sometimes
you tumble past your car back to the highway.
You hear blue jays recite your name backwards in the juniper,
but you keep rumbling with gravity. You roll back
into town, and spin recklessly around a curve, tumbling
down Main. You pass Jimmy just home from Vietnam,
and your mother clothes-pinning sheets in the sun.
You tumble past your brothers playing baseball
behind the Point Brewery and your sister whispering secrets
in front of Woolworths. The scent of greasy
burgers wafts from the open door. You reach out to grab
old friends, but their fingers come off in your grip,
and now you are somersaulting down Iverson Hill.
The momentum reaches a crescendo. You are a musical
note piercing the sound barrier. Gravity has you in the thick
of its fingers. Dawn sheds graffiti on your battered
limbs as you somersault over the Wisconsin Street Bridge
and come to a halt Sunday morning on the freshly
poured sidewalk of Saint Stephen's Church. Father McGinley
blesses you with holy water. Sister Veronica washes
your wounds. You leave an imprint of your face in concrete.

Zimbabwean Stone Sculptures

Loveland Museum and Gallery

When rocks come alive the feather of the owl will trace its way
back to the song of the ancestral. The malachite bowl
will claim its mother and bury its earthen face into her pebbled
skirt. When rocks rub the sleep from their eyes, the fish
will swallow one another, rocks will stretch their tired arms,
their feet will resemble something I am not supposed to touch.

When rocks come alive Zimbabwe will know its children, the texture
of jade, jasper, orange quartz. Their tongues will form crystals.
Their eyes will memorize the sound of tambourines, rain on a thatched
roof. When rocks rub sleep from their eyes, their copper muscles
will shimmer with bare feet on dusty roads. When rocks stretch
their awakening arms, the eye of the sculptor will swivel on its axis.

When rocks come alive, the raptor will call sandstone its mother.
A malachite voice will rise from seven mouths. A Zimbabwean
father will carry his own father to market. When rocks wake from sleep
one will accuse the other, *You have stolen my eggs.* The other
will reply, *We are living in good health.* When rocks stretch their muscled
arms, my hand will reach out to touch black onyx as if it were asleep.

Though I've Never Heard a Raven Speak

I've memorized their alphabet of latitude, turquoise
glint of eye, grey lisp of underwing. I mimic

and they follow, swooping inches from my ear, ravens
cawing in their blend of romance languages.

Though I've never heard a raven speak, I've warned
them of the parrot quoting *Nevermore* in Poe's first draft.

I've warned them of brushstrokes in Picasso's *Guernica,*
the anaphora of burnt cities: Pearl Harbor, Hiroshima, Falluja.

Though I've never heard a raven speak, I tell them my story:
Chasing my sister across the carpet, I tagged her. A small flame

*burst on the back of her neck. We held out our fingers and watched
a spark leap. Then we tried it with kisses. A tiny flame ignited*

between our lips. Though I've never heard a raven speak,
I tell them fear is not an orphan. There are tornados in every sky.

Each river has its flood. They remind me if disappointment
were fatal, the survivors would all be optimists, people with raven

power walking through snowfields talking to wingspan, people
crossing alfalfa stubble, fingers emitting sparks, people hungry

for what they are igniting. Though I've never heard a raven
speak, I've seen their ink unfetter sky, their vocabulary endless.

Primary Hue

I want to read poetry that sheds its skin
and leaves translucence lying on the back step.
I want to read starlings, excited birds that chatter
above my head, shuffling through pages of juniper.
I don't know foreign alphabets or strange insects.
I only know the flutter at the window
when the light goes out
               and the moth has no center,
like my mother's dementia. *I remember my neck,* she says,
propping her chin in the hammock of her hands,
while I compare the color red to the color red,
trace the burgundy lines of tallow waxed to the kitchen table,
read about medieval castles, their maroon tapestries
strung from doorposts.
               I can read all the parts of red.
It starts with an open vein and ends in the Sangre de Cristo sunset
streaked with pale pink, burgundy, maroon, berry-berry,
classic red, double mocha until I think I am describing lipstick,
and choose process narration. I paint my mother's nails
and her lips to match,
               dip the brush in pink coral and stroke
its tiny bristles over her thumbnail, twist the tube marked 'Rose'
and stroke her upper lip. I don't conceal anything,
just keep on stroking until I get cause and effect,
until the color of wine tints my memory, until the gypsy moth
clings to the night shade,
               until nothing but red frames the blue opal
of her necklace, and the owl picks up the snake skins,
one by one, wings them away, and I am left
with a familiar alphabet stringing the margin,
the feet of crane flies clutching the screen.

Lluvía Huérfana

I am relearning snow with its single
name. Today it is weighted and warm,
melting tracks behind my skis
—soft wood, blue wax, white memory.
    Lluvía, casí
Under a sky struggling with robins
their flight so low they are pressed
towards earth and me, how their wings
mingle with my visible breath.
    Casí lluvía
There is water in every language.
It's how memory survives.
Like rain spreading across the *llano*
filling the arroyo with casual bantering,
    Lluvía de nuevo
Like the *Huajatolla,* breasts of the earth,
covered in white, snowmelt sashaying
her liquid promise through these foothills
—run-off and the orphan rain.
    Lluvía otra vez
Like two sisters, sipping *agua de sandía*
through paper straws, pacing words
between them, connecting
with the wound their arguments make.
    Lluvía por supuesto
Like the juniper struggling with difficult
snow, splitting finally to expose
the white underwood, how
the severed bough changes from
green to rust in a single season.
    Lluvía siempre

Three Wishes

I gave my magic to my daughter, covered her
with blue ink at birth, gave her spoons and vowels,
gave her tonsils and voice. I gave my magic
to my daughter, filled her bassinet with pens, boots,
notebooks, I gave my magic to my daughter,
filled her veins with ink, her mouth with alphabet.

My pen tastes like bitter porcelain, like manganese,
nickel, like scorched metal, smells like hot
tar, burnt cedar, smells like smoke rings. I gave
my pen to my daughter so she can draw a straight
line to my mother, so she can sketch a woman's
laughter on the last page next to my father's cigar.

My boots smell like deep grass, crushed snow,
smell like swamp moss, lake minnows. I gave my boots
to my daughter, the taste of leather on her tongue
and in her nostrils the smell of my father's cigar,
to my daughter so she can crush leaves underfoot,
so she can hike into winter, snowboard on her back.

My notebook tastes like pitted cherries, Vermouth,
tastes like papyrus, a hint of lime. My notebook smells
like vanilla and sweat, like butterflies, traffic fumes, wisteria
and charcoal. I gave my notebook to my daughter so she
can inhale exhaust, speak Portuguese, so she can hear wings,
to my daughter so she can smell smoke and scribble love notes.

I gave my magic to my daughter—my pen, boots,
notebook. My daughter lost my pen in the river,
in murky water, cattails, bullfrogs. She lost my boots in traffic,
in car exhaust. She lost my boots to hot asphalt and burnt
tar. She lost my notebook to the Tower of Babel, lost
my notebook to seven languages and an apostrophe.

Notes from the Cabin

Even the trees have a hidden agenda,
their patient wood, the rawness
of their leaves, the tenderness they harbor.
The solitary crow barks its departure
from the open window. Yesterday a water
spider discovered my leg as I waded
through the dark mulch of nutrients. A turtle
slid off its log and the muskrat lifted
one curious eye above water. I am erecting
a dock through marsh. The muskrat
is uneasy. She burrows deeper into shoreline.
Security has taken on a shade of dementia.
Burrow deeper. Swim with caution. I'll call
that sandy spot *Beach* and go there often.
I'll sit back camouflaged by swamp grass,
memorize the viridian of bullfrogs mating.

We were eating at the pine table
when the storm came. We were sitting
next to the glass window watching
grey water translate itself into white
froth, almost like anger. My sister
told me she was *let go* after
twenty-five years of teaching, *let go*
like a fish that was too small or too big,
or just not. I simply replied *Be careful,*
knowing she has a short history
of cell division mutated into the Big C.
I was fishing the day she was diagnosed.
My daughter passed me the box
of worms and I injected one with my hook.
I fished while the muskrat nursed
her young and the spider fed on plant lice.
I waited patiently for that tension
at the end of an invisible line.

I've seen the pine snake uncoil and slip
into the murky shallow as if it were
a loose thread set adrift by complicated
wind. I am just as silent waiting
for language to cross my baited pen,
ink scrawl, the angleworm of my restless
soul. This is where the color green
was born, where the tenacity of flies
goes undisputed, where the lake's
cornucopia of dark matter feeds my presence
and that of passing minnows.

An emerald cold rises from the swamp
like an airy fog eliminating mosquitoes
and water spiders. The turtle has submerged
and the muskrat curls in her earthen den.
I am left with still water, my toes immersed
in this murky celadon. I sketch
cattails, their myriad stems, their open husks,
the loss of their downy interiors drifting
on musk air. This is the myth of swamp,
its exaggerated breath, so like the jet stream
unfolding layer after layer of consciousness.

I thought it was mice at first, their leavings
sprinkled across my deck. Then I saw
their wings, satin black. But I grew
to anticipate their presence, how at dusk
they swept the sky for mosquitoes, their dark
wings crisscrossing over the swamp's
nostalgic voice. I sat on the dock, listened
to their radiating assonance, until
the croaking of bullfrogs drowned them out
and the night's viridian absorbed them.

When Anna Meets for Lunch

We wash our hands in daughters
over platters of oranges and saffron
over spices turned yellow by steam.

We lift the latch of yesterday, let
the dead husband bring cattails into the living room,
place them in salt water and brine.

We were born with *100% cotton* on the neck label,
a penny between our teeth, lips of marbled granite,
our ten perfect fingers pressing the vulva of dissidence.

We are women together when the corrals want only men.
We ride three-legged bulls. Ours is a time full of thistle
and rose milk, the sticky essence of fingertips.

We are the shadows in a room without baskets or spoons,
always pressing our ear to the wall. We fill our days with students
dressed in consonants, their fingers full of history.

We know Saturday night for what it really is, a hoax
dressed in aluminum slippers. We pray for marbled rain,
its knuckles denting the hoods of jeeps.

We are pearls born in the clam's lust for sand. We are
coal before the diamond. What can pressure make of us now,
taking us by the hand into the kaleidoscope of dark?

Acknowledgments

I am grateful to the following publications in which these poems or earlier versions of these poems first appeared:

Adobe Walls: New Mexico Anthology: "Turistas: El Museo de las Momias," "Framing a Piece of Ruin," "From the Coast of Almería," "Kiss," *"La Playa"*

Big Muddy: "A Labyrinth of Moons," *"Pozo Cañada"*

Blue Mesa Review: "Albino King Snake"

Cider Press Review: "My Hand through the Keyhole"

The Eleventh Muse: "green," *"Lluvia Huérfana"* as *"Huerfano* Rain"

Ellipsis Literature and Art: "Love Story," "Rash from the Corn Mold Crepes," "Onions"

Green Mountains Review: "The Dream Turtle" as "The Sea Turtle"

Hunger Mountain: "What Does Lorca Own?" *(Winner of the 2007 Ruth Stone Prize)*

Kestrel: "Driving Away"

Margie: "Gravity II"

Nimrod International Journal: "Woman Resting" *(Finalist, 2011 Pablo Neruda Prize),* "Shaking the Kaleidoscope" *(Semi-Finalist, 2007 Pablo Neruda Prize),* "When I Clap"

Pilgrimage: "Assassination"

Plainsongs: "My Mother's Dance" *(A Plainsongs Award Poem)*

The Pinch: "Lunatic," "Zimbabwe Stone Structures"

Puerto del Sol: "Dusting"

Rattle: "History of My Body," "Primary Hue"

Runes: "Notes from the Cabin"

Southwestern American Literature: "Aztec Exhibit: The World of Motecuhzoma"

Sugar House Review: "After Reading *Romance Sonámbulo,"* "Concourse A Exhibit," "Though I've Never Heard a Raven Speak"

Weber Studies: "Finger-Birds," "Fish Like Angels"

Words and Images: "Argil: Pure Clay," "In the Beginning," "Gravity I," "Neruda" *(Second Place, Stephen Dunn Poetry Award)*

I would like to thank Fundación Valparaíso, the Helene Wurlitzer Foundation, the Harwood Museum, Jentel, Ucross, the Vermont Studio Center, Colorado Art Ranch, and the Anderson Center for their fellowship residencies, as well as the San Miguel Poetry Week Conference where I was recipient of the W.D. Snodgrass Award for Poetic Endeavor and Excellence.

My appreciation also goes to the editors of Main Street Rag Publishing for publication of the poetry collection *In My Dreams Neruda* as an editor's choice, to the editors of White Eagle Coffee Store Press for the publication of *El Río de las Ánimas Perdidas en Purgatorio* as a winner in the WECS Press Poetry Chapbook Award, and to Outlaw Artists Press for the publication of the poetry collection, *Unwritten Letters.*

My appreciation extends to the following individuals who were instrumental in bringing this book to its final presentation:

Jennifer Clement, Mary Crow, Robin Greene, Christine Holbert, Richard Jackson, Susan Mitchell, Nancy Takacs, Leslie Ullman, and Carolyne Wright. A special thank you also to the Colrain Poetry Manuscript Conference, Oaxaca Women's Writing Retreat, and the Vermont College of Fine Arts Postgraduate Writers' Conference.